POPPEOPLE™

Destiny's Child!

by Eartha Glass

SCHOLASTIC INC.

New York   Toronto   London   Auckland   Sydney   Mexico City   New Delhi   Hong Kong   Buenos Aires

Photo Credits

Front cover: Todd Kaplan/Star File Photo; Back cover: Fabrice Trombert/Retna Ltd.; Page 1: Steve Granitz/Retna Ltd.; Page 2: (bottom) Steve Granitz/Retna Ltd.; Pages 3, 4, 5: Paul Fenton; Page 6: Jeffrey Mayer/Star File Photo; Page 7: Rikken/Sunshine/Retna U.K.; Page 8: Anthony Dixon/Lfi-UDIX.

ISBN 0-439-32695-8

Designed by Peter Koblish
Photo Editor: Sharon Lennon

12 11 10 9 8 7 6 5 4 3 2 1   1 2 3 4 5 6/0
Printed in the U.S.A.
First Scholastic printing, October 2001

CONTENTS PAGE

INTRODUCTION

If there's one female group that's been hitting it hard, it's the sizzling trio Destiny's Child. Beyoncé Knowles, Kelly Rowland, and Michelle Williams have won award after award and scored hit song after hit song. And guess what? They're just getting warmed up! So sit back and come along for the ride!

Flashback to 1998: Destiny's Child started gaining a fan following with the catchy single "No, No, No" from their debut disc. Their next album, *The Writing's on the Wall,* was jam-packed with fresh R&B tracks that showcased the girls' intense, tight harmonies. The album spawned not one or two but *four* number one singles: "Say My Name," "Bills, Bills, Bills," "Bug A Boo" and "Jumpin' Jumpin'." How's that for gettin' busy?

If you haven't guessed by now, Destiny's Child

1

likes to keep things high energy! Instead of taking a break, the gals stoked the flames and came out with "Independent Women Part 1." The uplifting, soulful track was featured on the soundtrack for *Charlie's Angels* starring Drew Barrymore, Cameron Diaz, and Lucy Liu. "Independent" is still getting plenty of airplay, too. Its groovy beats and positive lyrics are hard to resist!

Now, just when you thought things might start winding down for Destiny's Child, no way! Along came another album from the gorgeous threesome! It's called *Survivor* and Beyoncé, Michelle, and Kelly "premiered" the first single, "Survivor," a few times on various award shows in early 2001.

Survivor is the first album for Kelly, Michelle, and Beyoncé as a trio. Some members came and went along the way, but the girls say that this lineup is solid and good to go. They've already hit the tour circuit with the new songs from *Survivor* and are having a great time!

As the saying goes, the third one's the charm and D.C.'s third CD is doing much more than just surviving the charts. It's kickin' it hard! You can bet *Survivor* is set to break records for sure, 'cause any way you look at it, Destiny's Child is destined for success! Big time!

CHAPTER 1
Survivin' the Heat

When Destiny's Child performed their brand-spankin'-new single "Survivor" on the 2001 Grammys and Soul Train Awards, they were just a tad nervous! There were the new lyrics to remember, slick dance moves, not to mention the girls were up for several awards! Talk about tummy butterflies!

Still, as Beyoncé, Michelle, and Kelly unveiled "Survivor," they weren't worried about whether or not they were going to take home an award. Instead, the ladies were totally focused on giving the performance of their lives. And did they deliver!

Not only can these girls sing, they can groove, they can strut! Needless to say, *Survivor*, which debuted back in May 2001, rocked the charts. And why not? It's got slammin' tracks with that *hot*

R&B urban sound that Destiny's Child made so famous!

While *you're* singing along to "Emotion" now, your mom and dad may have gotten groovy to the song way back. In the 1970s, disco superstars the Bee Gees wrote "Emotion." Originally sung by Samantha Sang, it was a huge hit back in 1978. Beyoncé told MTV that the arrangement on "Emotion" is really great because of the acoustic guitar and the fact that she, Michelle, and Kelly each have their own verse. It was a perfect choice for Destiny's Child. "Thank you for writing that song, Bee Gees," said Beyoncé. "Y'all is tight." You can bet that Bee Gees songwriters Maurice and Barry Gibb were thrilled with Destiny's Child's modern R&B grooves on "Emotion." Talk about bringing disco into the new millennium and rocketing it up the charts!

Wonderin' how Beyoncé, Kelly, and Michelle managed to pencil in studio time to record *Survivor*? After all, they had a busy year in 2001 with all the magazine covers they appeared on, awards shows, and charity events they did. Backstage at the Grammy Awards Kelly said that they just went into the studio, rock and rolled and prayed that everything was going to be okay. Well, things turned out a little better than *okay*, wouldn't you say?

On *Survivor*, Beyoncé, Kelly, and Michelle do what they do best — use those awesome voices! Hardcore Destiny's Child fans won't be disappointed with the hip-hop flavored melodies. Plus, if you liked "Independent Women" and "Jumpin' Jumpin'" then you're in for a real treat 'cause you get to hear a lot more from Beyoncé in the songwriting department on the new album. She wrote a good deal of the material on *Survivor*, including the title track.

Lyrically, the girls have said that there is one small shift. On *Survivor*, they've lightened up on the fellas a bit. Of course, guys everywhere are thrilled about that little change!

Something that gals (and guys) dig about past Destiny's Child songs is that they were packed with go-for-it lyrics that made you feel you could make it over the bumps in life. *Survivor* is no different. "A lot of the songs on this album are very inspirational," said Kelly. "Empowering" is the word Michelle used to describe the vibe on *Survivor*. No surprise, 'cause keeping the faith and having a positive outlook on life have always been at the root of the group. You'd better believe D.C. had to stay super-positive when they were just starting out. They held tight to their dreams until success came a knockin'!

Beyoncé said in a past interview that there were some people in Houston, their hometown, who said the girls were wasting their time trying to get a record deal because no one from there had ever done it before. Well, with hard work and dedication, Destiny's Child proved them wrong! "We are proof that whatever you put your mind to, you can achieve," said Beyoncé. "This is just the start for us."

And what a start it has been! These Houston honeys have proven that they are here to stay. Is anyone complaining? No way! Destiny's Child is an inspiration for the whole world. They've reminded everyone about the power of faith — if you really believe in a dream, it can come true!

The girls take their jobs seriously and try to make every effort to reach their fans. You can expect 110 percent from Destiny's Child whenever the group gets involved with something, whether it's a big project or something on the smaller scale. They absolutely dig singing and are so happy that their music is being accepted. They feel blessed and promise that they'll do their best to keep up the good work!

Heads Up — More to Come!

As for what's in the works, expect lots more singles from the talented trio. Be sure to pick up all the cool and hip mixes of your fave *Survivor* tracks as they are recorded and released as maxi-singles.

Also, be on the lookout for a Destiny's Child DVD. It'll feature awesome concert footage of Beyoncé, Michelle, and Kelly kickin' it onstage as well as the super-hot videos to such smashes as "Say My Name." Sounds delicious!

On the solo project front, Beyoncé stars as Carmen in MTV's *Carmen: A Hip Hopera*. The original telefilm is a hip-hop update of the opera *Carmen* by Georges Bizet. Set in modern day Philly, the MTV movie focuses on the romance between Carmen and Sgt. Derrick Hill (played by Mekhi Phifer). In the original opera, Carmen is a factory worker who falls for a soldier named Don José. *Carmen* has been updated twice before — once as a musical and once as the movie *Carmen Jones* starring Dorothy Dandridge and Harry Belafonte. This time around there is narration by rapper Da Brat as well as plenty of hot hip-hop songs. *Carmen: A Hip Hopera* aired in May on MTV. Also look for all three ladies getting involved with more projects that, like *Carmen*, challenge their creative spirits!

If that's not enough, get ready to see the luscious ladies on TV and in magazine ads — from head to toe! Beyoncé's first commercial already aired back in the spring. It was for L'Oréal and boy, is she worth it! Beyoncé signed a contract to be a spokesperson for L'Oréal Paris and said she couldn't believe she was going to be one of the L'Oréal ladies. She had a blast and is looking forward to filming her next commercial real soon.

Destiny's Child has also teamed up with Candie's shoes. Beyoncé, Michelle, and Kelly are set to appear in Candie's spring and fall 2001 print and multimedia ad campaigns. The trio has also signed on to help launch Candie's Retro, a collection of sandals inspired by the 1980s. The D.C. ladies love Candie's shoes and said that they were flattered to be chosen to help launch the new vintage line. "Candie's is all about being sexy, fun, and independent, and that's how we view ourselves," said Beyoncé. The D.C. gals are in pretty good company, too! Other spokespeople for Candie's include Sugar

Ray's Mark McGrath, L'il Kim, Brandy, and Shania Twain.

As if that weren't enough, Destiny's Child is also slated to perform a live concert for Candie's customers and make two in-store appearances. You can also log onto candies.com and look for an upcoming live chat with Destiny's Child. Candie's is also planning to give away hundreds — repeat hundreds! — of tickets during D.C.'s 2001 tour and also hold a contest where one lucky winner plus a friend can win a free trip to Destiny's Child's next video shoot! Is that too cool, or what? So make sure you log onto candies.com and keep informed of all these and other Destiny's Child happenings!

A Dream Come True

Michelle, Beyoncé, and Kelly all know how important it is to hold onto your dreams. If they had given up on their music career after a few disappointments, then the world might not have ever heard the awesome music of Destiny's Child today! It's a good thing the gals stuck with it and survived the past few years. Michelle told reporters shortly before the group's third album *Survivor* was released, "The year 2000 was very challenging for Destiny's

Child, and I know that gave Beyoncé a lot of inspiration to write the song 'Survivor.'" So even when things don't seem to be going your way, just remember that they will soon enough if you hang tough! Use the space below to write down some of the hopes and dreams that you'd like to fulfill some day. Reach for the stars!

1. _____

2. _____

3. _____

4. _____

5. _____

6. _____

7. _____

8. _____

9. _____

10. _____

CHAPTER 2
Destined for Success

Ever since they were toddlers, Beyoncé, Michelle, and Kelly were really into music. They all loved singing in church and even pretended they were stars at home. So it should come as no surprise to their friends and family that they've officially "made it," because they grew up hearing all about the girls' dreams to be singers someday.

The roots of Destiny's Child can be traced back to 1990. Beyoncé was singing in talent shows before she hooked up with LaTavia Roberson at the age of eight. The two were the first members of Destiny's Child. In 1992, Kelly, Beyoncé's cousin, joined up. Story has it that Kelly was overheard singing Whitney Houston's "I'm Your Baby Tonight" and she was urged to try out for the group. She did and made the cut! Then, a year later, Beyoncé met LeToya Luckett while the two were in the Girl Scouts (they used to sell Girl Scout cookies together!). After LeToya tried out and was invited to join, the first lineup of Destiny's Child was underway.

Though the girls were only nine and ten years old at the time, it wasn't long before they started getting attention! As a foursome, the girls were invited to appear on *Star Search* in 1992. Though they only had one song that was rap, the girls were asked to do a rap song for the competition in the hip-hop category. "It wasn't our best song, but we did it," said Beyoncé, looking back on it. The girls didn't win, but they sure did learn a lot from their experience. Beyoncé said that the timing wasn't really right for the group and that it even might have been too soon if their careers had skyrocketed just then. She said that they might not have appreciated their success as much if it had happened when they were so young. One majorly important lesson the girls learned was that they just had to keep their dream alive. They knew they could make it!

They also had a lot of fun! It wasn't all work for the girls when they left Houston for Orlando, Florida, to audition for *Star Search*. The foursome was psyched for their first TV appearance, but they also had some excitement riding their bikes around the grounds of the resort where they stayed. Beyoncé recalled that at the time, she couldn't ride a bike very well and she had a hard time keeping up with the rest of the group. But she's a go-getter and she ended up doing just fine! Beyoncé said the whole trip was an adventure that she and Kelly will never ever forget!

After the girls returned to Texas and the excitement of *Star Search* settled down, they decided to put a hold on the rapping and take their music more in the direction of R&B with a dash of hip-hop. Right about then, Beyoncé's father, Mathew Knowles, came in full-time as the group's manager. The girls went to school by day, and in their off time spent their energies on perfecting the sound and style of Destiny's Child. They took every opportunity they could to perform in and around Houston. Their audiences included both young and older fans, and soon they were getting a good vibe going about Destiny's Child.

Following their appearance on *Star Search*, Destiny's Child landed gigs opening for such major acts as SWV (Sisters With Voices) and Dru Hill. As they honed their vocal harmonies, dance moves, and stage presence, the momentum was starting to build. Some more good news was on the way!

Opportunity came knocking again after the girls performed at the "Juneteenth Festival, The Black Expo" in Houston. Soon afterward, the girls were offered a record contract by Elektra Records. They thought it was their big break, but were bummed when the deal never panned out. If you can believe it, some naysayers took the opportunity to whisper that Destiny's Child was never going to get a record deal. Since the girls were so young, some people just didn't take them seriously. Still, the D.C. girls kept their chins up and continued to juggle schoolwork with their music.

"We had some major disappointments," Kelly admits, "but they only made us stronger and more determined than ever to make it. Plus, we all believe in God, and know that He's always been on our side."

In 1996, Columbia Records stepped up and offered the girls a brand-new contract. Beyoncé said in an interview that the folks at Columbia had actually been keeping an eye on the group since way back when. This time around, the deal went through as smooth as silk, and the girls were finally on their way to recording their debut album —

hooray! You better believe they were jumpin' jumpin' up and down with excitement!

Beyoncé cites that time as a major turning point in their careers. She says that when the time came to make their album, the girls never looked back! The Houston foursome was just so glad to finally have the opportunity that all of the problems of the past seemed to disappear.

And They're Off . . .

From the start, Columbia Records has been behind the group one hundred percent. Recognizing the incredible strength and talent of Destiny's Child, the label decided to release their first single, "Killing Time," on the Columbia soundtrack for the film *Men in Black*. It proved a good decision because as Destiny's Child finished recording the rest of their self-titled debut, "Killing Time" was already waking the world up to their stunning voices and fresh urban sound. Talk about an impressive intro!

By the time *Destiny's Child* came out in 1998, "Killing Time" was enjoying a nice stint on the charts and the buzz was going strong! The lead single from the debut was "No, No, No" and was received with open arms from the already HUGE

Destiny's Child fan base. The jammin' "No, No, No" featured Wyclef Jean of the Fugees and was a smash for Destiny's Child all around! It not only hit the top ten in the U.S. but also in the U.K.! It was soon followed by the moving "With Me" and the single "Get on the Bus," which was actually featured on the soundtrack for the flick *Why Do Fools Fall in Love?*

Not wanting to break their stride, Destiny's Child soon followed their debut with *The Writing's on the Wall*. It didn't take long for singles off this CD to start chartin' either! "Bills, Bills, Bills" was a hip and tight little number that shook a finger at the fellas (and gals!) who took to slackin' once a romance took off. Kevin "She'kspere" Briggs, who was also behind TLC's "No Scrubs," produced the song. "Bills, Bills, Bills" was hot-hot-hot and it quickly became the first number one single for Destiny's Child!

It looked like everything was just peachy, but like most roads in life, the road to success for Destiny's Child was not always perfectly smooth. There have been some bumps along the way too.

As the group was touring to support *The Writing's on the Wall* in 2000, the first of two lineup changes took place. LeToya and LaTavia parted ways with Destiny's Child. This could have very well brought the destiny of Destiny's Child to a screeching halt.

Beyoncé later told a music magazine that it was a scary time. Still, she and Kelly refused to let some lineup changes break up the whole group. Being such a big fan of music herself, Beyoncé always felt badly when her fave groups broke up just because of one or two changes. She always thought it would be cool to see what would have happened if the remaining members carried on.

Their schedule was packed, and Kelly and Beyoncé didn't want to have to cancel any appearances and let any fans down. So, they actually carried on and did several shows by themselves. You can bet it was different and maybe even a little scary for Beyoncé and Kelly to be up there by themselves! But once they started singing and saw how much joy their voices and music brought their fans, they decided that they were going to stick together no matter what! They weren't going to let *anything* tear them apart!

So the girls hustled, and along with their manager and the recommendations of friends, the two openings were quickly filled by Michelle Williams and Farrah Franklin.

Michelle had been a backup singer for Monica, and had the voice of an angel. She was also no stranger to the busy and sometimes tiring life of sticking to a tour schedule. Farrah, a dancer, was actually an extra at the video shoot for "Bills, Bills, Bills." Kelly and Beyoncé had stayed in touch with her after they had met in Los Angeles.

The New Destiny's Child

First on the list for the new foursome was to go and shoot a music video. Within hours of joining the group, Michelle and Farrah headed with Beyoncé and Kelly to shoot the video for "Say My Name." Now that's getting down to business!

"It was a very exciting feeling," recalls Michelle. At first, she was very nervous. After all, she not only had to sing, but also dance — in front of a camera, director, and tons of crew members! But Beyoncé and Kelly gave her lots of support and totally believed in her. In the end, the video was complete and everything worked out just great. If you've ever seen it on MTV, then you know it's as awesome and hot as the song!

The girls were quickly rewarded, too, because the groovy "Say My Name" peaked at number one on the music charts and virtually made Destiny's Child a household name! It received plenty of backup from the single "Jumpin' Jumpin'," which also started racing up the charts right behind it.

But there was one more change on the Destiny's Child horizon. A short while after the girls shot the video for "Jumpin' Jumpin'," Farrah parted ways with the group. The personnel change came that summer and it was a bit of a shock to Beyoncé, Kelly, and Michelle. As they toyed with the idea of finding a replacement, Beyoncé, Kelly, and Michelle were a little bummed. Soon enough, the three bucked up and after getting lots of support from family members, friends, and fans, they started thinking positive again!

They rethought their sound vocally and decided that Michelle's voice was such a strong asset to the group that it'd be all right to keep Destiny's Child as a trio. With each performance their harmonies and stage presence became tighter and smoother.

Back when they were starting out, Destiny's Child had a motto: "Much prayer, much power. No prayer, no power. And a group that prays together, stays together." They never forgot it and they drew on their spiritual strengths to help see them through the rough spots. "The group is now at its emotional, spiritual, and vocal best," Beyoncé said in a magazine interview.

Right now, Destiny's Child stands rock solid as a trio. Beyoncé says that Destiny's Child with Michelle "feels real." The bottom line is, the three of them are all in sync and they couldn't be happier!

Besides, they didn't have much time to stay glum 'cause come fall of last year, the soundtrack for the action film *Charlie's Angels* was released and the Beyoncé-penned single "Independent Women Part I" started rocketing up the charts! As the gals performed at NBC's *Christmas in Rockefeller Center* on November 29 along with Natalie Cole, Marc Anthony, and 98° to accompany the lighting of the Big Apple's Christmas tree, "Independent Women Part I" was lighting up the charts at numero uno! "Independent" was still there in January 2001, too. What a way to ring in the New Year, eh?!

With the release of *Survivor*, their name is still hanging out on the charts and well, all over the place! Despite the bumps, the ride is not over yet, 'cause this trio of lovelies is just getting revved up! And you'd better believe they're destined to survive!

Thinking of Starting a Group of Your Own?

As you've just read, success didn't happen over-
night for Destiny's Child. They worked at it long
and hard. They didn't put school on the back
burner, either, just because they had a dream. They
stayed focused on graduating from high school
while at the same time, they set their sights on
singing and improving as performers. In the end,
they are living proof that with faith and dedication,
dreams do in fact come true! So if you've been day-
dreaming in class about being in a band some day,
then you'd better check out this checklist to get you
organized and on your way. Jot your answers down
after the questions and start makin' it happen. Hey,
everybody's got to start somewhere!

1. First things first. Who are the MEMBERS of
your group? Write their names down here. You can
also come up with nicknames for the members.

_____   _____

_____   _____

_____   _____

_____   _____

2. Which VOCAL part will each member sing? For example, who will sing lead vocals and who will sing backup? Of course everyone in the group can sing lead vocals. That's what Beyoncé, Kelly, and Michelle did on *Survivor*!

_____   _____

_____   _____

_____   _____

_____   _____

3. Do any of the members play any INSTRU-MENTS? If so, write down which member plays which instrument here. Don't sweat it if no one in your group plays the guitar or drums, etc. Destiny's Child once said that their voices were their instruments!

_____   _____

_____   _____

_____   _____

_____   _____

4. Next on the list is a cool NAME for your group. Destiny's Child was inspired from a passage in the Bible, so be creative! Sit down with the other members and come up with some possible names for your music group. Then jot the names down here

and take a vote. If you are deadlocked or can't decide, you might want to get a little help from your classmates and run a poll in the school newspaper!

_____   _____

_____   _____

_____   _____

_____   _____

5. What are some of the MUSIC and SOUNDS that you and the rest of the members admire? All the girls in Destiny's Child really looked up to the Supremes and Diana Ross. They also shared a love for lots of other R&B bands and gospel music. It's kind of important that the members in your group are fairly in sync when it comes to sound. You don't want someone who thinks hard rock is the road when everyone else grooves on ballads! Write down some of your fave groups and/or styles of music here and see if they jibe.

_____   _____

_____   _____

_____   _____

6. What will the LOOK of your group be like? Destiny's Child often wear similar outfits so everyone

can tell they're together in a group. The Spice Girls, however, tended to each dress differently. What do you think would be some cool style ideas for your group that will make you stand out?

_____   _____

_____   _____

_____   _____

_____   _____

7. Beyoncé wrote a good bulk of the material on *Survivor*. The experiences of her life and those of Michelle and Kelly inspired her lyrics. One person can write the SONGS for your group, or everyone can share this job. What will be some of the ideas you and the other members would like to explore in your lyrics?

_____   _____

_____   _____

_____   _____

_____   _____

8. And last but definitely not least, what will be the general MESSAGE of the music that you and your group will strive to make? If you had to use one word to describe the message Destiny's Child puts out there, it would have to be "empowerment" or

"independence." Write down the message you and your pals hope to send with the music that you make.

_____   _____

_____   _____

_____   _____

_____   _____

CHAPTER 3
Crossin' Bridges, Winnin' Awards

Take one look at the photos in this book and you'll see that Beyoncé, Kelly, and Michelle are standing tall and confident. They've got plenty to be proud of, too, having been honored so many times and in so many ways. Get a load of some of Destiny's Child's past awards and achievements!

This year started off perfectly for the three-some. On January 8, 2001, they walked away with an American Music Award for Favorite Soul/R&B Group. It was the first time for this category, and the girls were all smiles! During their acceptance speech at the American Music Awards, the trio started off by thanking God and ended with thanking their fans. Said Kelly, "And finally, the fans — thank you for helping Destiny's Child survive the year 2000. God bless you."

Next, at the 43rd Grammy Awards in February, Destiny's Child was nominated for five Grammys, including Record of the Year and Song of the Year for "Say My Name." The girls won a total of two Grammys on the star-studded night — one for Best R&B Performance by a Duo or Group With Vocal for "Say My Name" and one for Best R&B Song for "Say My Name."

At the NAACP's 32nd Annual Image Awards, Destiny's Child won for Outstanding Duo or Group for "Say My Name." It was a real honor for Beyoncé, Michelle, and Kelly because to receive an Image Award means you're getting a gigantic thumbs up for being positive role models for young people everywhere! The girls were thrilled!

A few days later, at the 2001 Soul Train Music Awards, Destiny's Child was honored again by being chosen for the Sammy Davis, Jr. Award for Entertainer of the Year, Female. The girls had the double joy of being presented the award by Wyclef Jean. They are huge fans of Wyclef's music, not to mention they're also good chums! If you remember, Wyclef was partially responsible for the fly production of D.C.'s debut album, and he's also featured on "No, No, No Part 2" and "Illusion." Wyclef was really psyched for the ladies, 'cause he's been a Destiny's Child supporter since the very beginning!

As if all these awards aren't enough, other Destiny's Child achievements include four *Billboard* Music Awards including Artist of the Year, two Soul Train Lady of Soul Awards including Best R&B Album of the Year (Group) for *The Writing's on the Wall*, and an MTV Video Music Award! And this isn't even counting all their other honors, such as performing at the Brit Awards, the U.K. version of the Grammys, as well as taking part in numerous charity events and benefits. Whew! And there's no question that the list will most definitely go on and on and on!

Gorgeous at the Grammys

The American Music Awards and Grammys were a great way for the trio to leave the bumps of 2000 behind and build a fantastic bridge to their bright and promising future. Rather than focusing on if they were going to get an award or not, the girls chose to focus on their performances at the shows. After all, their music is what brought them there in the first place!

When they were asked to perform at the Grammys this year, they were still in the studio hard at work trying to finish *Survivor*. The ladies thought it would be cool to do a few songs on the show, so they decided on a medley of "Say My Name" and "Independent Women Part I." It would be more work, of course, blending both songs and mixing the music, but the girls didn't mind. They wanted to do something different and fresh!

Actually, just to be asked to perform at the Grammys was honor enough for the girls. "We don't have to win anything," said Beyoncé before the show. "An acceptance speech takes like twenty seconds, a performance is four minutes." And what a four minutes it was! The girls stunned audiences with their powerful vocals, awesome moves, and sizzling good looks!

Backstage, the girls told reporters that though they were a little antsy about their performance, they were thrilled with how everything turned out. Michelle said that winning the two Grammys was a wonderful dream come true. When asked what it feels like waiting for the presenters to announce the winner, Beyoncé said, "Your heart just starts beating so fast, and when they call your name, you forget everything. It's weird!" Congratulations on all the wins, Destiny's Child!

A little later, when asked to perform at the Soul Train Awards, Beyoncé, Michelle, and Kelly decided to step into the future by showcasing the lead single off their new album. The song "Survivor" was still fairly new and you can bet they were nervous about it coming out okay. Everything went off fabulously, and both fans and their music peers were pumped for the release of *Survivor*.

The Story of *Survivor*

Give the *Survivor* CD a close listen, and you'll realize that Destiny's Child not only challenge themselves on stage, but in the studio as well. This time around, they hooked up with some top-notch producers, including Rodney Jerkins (he's worked with Britney Spears, Brandy, and lots of other megastars), former Tony! Toni! Toné! member Dwayne Wiggins, and newcomers Dent and Rod Sufari. Actually, Rodney and Dwayne have lent a helping hand on past D.C. albums. Beyoncé, who co-produced and co-wrote the Destiny's Child smash singles "Independent Women Part 1" and "Jumpin' Jumpin'," decided to go full blast on *Survivor* in those departments. "I actually produced and arranged the whole album, every song on there,"

30

she says. "Thank God the girls gave me the opportunity."

Much of the material on *Survivor* has uptempo vibes, cool bridges, and awesome lyrics that stay with you long after one listen. The music grooves on so many levels that it's hard not to start dancing to it.

Still, the girls weren't the least bit afraid to slow the beats down a bit on some of the tracks on *Survivor*. On the sweet-'n'-slower "Brown Eyes," they let their voices work their magic. The song was produced by Walter Afanasieff, who's worked with Mariah Carey and Celine Dion. It's a beautiful ballad that really allows Beyoncé, Michelle, and Kelly's radiant vocals to soar!

Destiny's Child also took some other major chances on *Survivor*. For instance, they suspected that "The Story of Beauty" might cause some controversy, but that didn't make Kelly, Beyoncé, and Michelle shy away! They chose the song because it shines some light on the problems some young people go through while growing up. It was actually inspired by a letter that Destiny's Child received from a fan. Michelle says that "The Story of Beauty" is a deep and touching song that lets you know you're beautiful inside no matter what.

That took a lot of courage and dedication, don't

you think? You bet! But Destiny's Child is totally cool like that! It's super-important for Beyoncé, Michelle, and Kelly to keep their music real, to keep growing as artists, and also to keep getting their message out there. They think it's great if their songs help build bridges of communication between generations. And if people start feeling more positive and empowered after listening to *Survivor*, well, you can be sure that makes Destiny's Child pretty happy, too!

"It's been a whirlwind for us, and we're hopeful that it will continue with our next album," said Beyoncé. Don't worry, ladies! You've proven that you're survivors and you're gonna make it!

An Honorable Mention for You!

Sounds as if Destiny's Child is going to need a whole room just to stash their many awards and trophies! Of course, they're not the only gals stackin' up the stars, are they? Surely you've nabbed some top honors, too! If you draw a blank, try answering some of the following questions:

Did you pass an exam with flying colors?
Did you ease up on that younger sibling lately?

Did you score big on your sports or cheerleading team?

Did you do a walkathon and raise money for charity?

Did you learn how to swim?

Did you win the spelling bee?

Did you do your chores without whining too much?

Did you land a part in the school play?

Did your home ec muffins simply melt in your mouth?

Did you get a spot on the school chorus or band?

Did you read a book that wasn't required by your teachers?

Did you do something nice for your family for no particular reason?

Now take a moment and reflect on all your splendid honors and achievements here. And as Michelle, Kelly, and Beyoncé will tell you, it doesn't matter if you win the award or not. It just matters that you gave it your best shot!

1. _____

2. _____

3. _____

4. _____

5. _____

6. _____

7. _____

8. _____

9. _____

10. _____

CHAPTER 4

A Song and a Prayer

Does Destiny's Child's music do wonders for your spirit? Does it make you want to sing and dance and pump your heart full of positive energy? Michelle, Beyoncé, and Kelly would be glad to hear that!

You see, all three ladies grew up with lots of spirituality and love. Kelly, Beyoncé, and Michelle were all brought up going to church and singing gospel music. Perhaps that explains in part their fantastic vocal harmonies that lift you right up to the heavens!

Ever since the group was first starting out back in the early nineties, Kelly and Beyoncé relied on the power of prayer to get them through any difficulties in life. And it wasn't just because their parents were dragging them either! Church became a

35

natural part of the group's schedule because they really enjoyed being there. If for some reason Kelly and Beyoncé couldn't make it on Sunday to the St. John's Methodist Church in Houston, then they both would feel a little bummed out. "We feel real empty when we don't go," Kelly told a magazine back in 1998.

"Dedication" should be Destiny's Child's middle name, 'cause as a lot of their pals were just chillin' watching TV and hitting the local theme parks, Kelly and Beyoncé were packing their summer days with all sorts of activities that were prepping them for a successful life in the music biz. In past interviews, the cousins have described it as a "summer camp" where days often began with a three-mile jog, followed by a full day of voice and dance practice. The group performed as much as they could in the summer, and during the school year, they often did one performance weekly.

When the group started turning heads, the girls got so busy that it was necessary to be home-schooled with tutors. They worked just as hard at home, too, having daily homework and tests.

Beyoncé and Kelly admit that the "camp" whipped them into shape. It also taught them plenty about discipline and how to manage a tight schedule. Certainly, it's one of the reasons these ladies are so professional and always make that extra effort to be on time!

As Beyoncé and Kelly were shaping up in Houston, up north in Chicago, Michelle was on a similar path, hoping to be a singer someday. She was also active in her family's local church and had a strong love of gospel music. Even at a young age, her voice was rich and powerful and stood out from the crowd.

When Michelle joined Destiny's Child last year, Beyoncé and Kelly said they both had a really good feeling about her. Michelle felt similarly and has expressed in interviews that she feels blessed to be a part of Destiny's Child. "It's been a wonderful year," Michelle said in a past interview. "Beyoncé and Kelly are the most talented ladies in the world. Despite everything that's gone on, we stuck together. God knew who He wanted to be in Destiny's Child."

This past March, when Destiny's Child attended the Image Awards to accept their trophy for Outstanding Group, they got a double treat! That same evening, famed gospel singer Yolanda Adams was honored with four awards including one for Outstanding Female Artist. The Destiny's Child ladies were thrilled to be sharing the same stage with the incredible gospel singer!

These days, Beyoncé, Michelle, and Kelly are sure to pack their Bibles when they hit the tour circuit. It's just one of the many ways that they stay connected not only to one another and their families but to their own souls! When the girls want to get focused quick, all they have to do is hold hands, say a prayer, and they're suddenly in sync! All three will vouch for the power of prayer.

So sure, the girls missed out on some things in their childhood, but as the saying goes, you can't have your cake and eat it too! Beyoncé, Kelly, and Michelle feel the sacrifices they made are well worth everything that they've gained. All three had big hopes of being successful singers and now that their dreams have come true, they are truly grateful and just couldn't be happier!

CHAPTER 5
Yes, Yes, Yes!

One of the reasons Beyoncé, Kelly, and Michelle decided to name their new album *Survivor* is because they jumped a few hurdles last year and survived with flying colors! How did they overcome the changes of going from a foursome to a threesome as well as juggle all their many responsibilities?

First off, stayin' positive definitely helps! The girls know that a clear head is necessary to not only make good decisions, but also for singing, songwriting, and performing. That's why they try to stay as focused as they can on the matter at hand. If their minds start to wander, they try their best to get back on track and stay with the program!

But how can they keep so cool when the pressure's on to deliver? Simple. They try to shrug that pressure right off their pretty shoulders! Beyoncé said that, of course, there is pressure, but the girls try not to focus on that. Otherwise, their creativity might suffer. They don't concern themselves with matching or beating the success of *The Writing's on the Wall* either. Instead, they try to just chill in the studio, have a little fun, and go with the flow of the music.

Secondly, Beyoncé, Kelly, and Michelle try to feel a happy vibe with everything they do. That good energy in turn gives them strength to face anything as a group and also individually.

One of the ways Michelle, Kelly, and Beyoncé keep the good vibrations coming is through communication. For example, if one of them is feeling down, then the other two are right behind her to give her a little pep talk or hug! You see, Beyoncé, Kelly, and Michelle are not only group mates, but they're best friends as well. It's not much different from when your best buds try to cheer you up by telling you something that they know will make you crack up, or maybe they just say, "You look great today!"

Their lives are a total whirlwind of activity and excitement, so the girls also talk to stay grounded and process everything that's happening to them every day. And that's quite a lot! All three women are very brave, but they also get courage from each other. That's how they're able to continue pushing the envelope creatively with their music as a trio and on their own.

Beyoncé, Kelly, and Michelle never, ever compete with one another. That would be silly because if one of the girls in the trio is looking her best and glowing, then that just makes the other two feel proud and look good too! In fact, they make it a point to help each other look and feel their absolute best. One thing's for sure, these women have got each others' backs!

This support also extends to their career choices and new opportunities that arise. When Beyoncé was asked to be the lead in MTV's *Carmen: A Hip Hopera*, Kelly and Michelle were behind her all the way and told her to go for it! Beyoncé said that she was a little nervous about signing on for the lead. As Carmen, she would not only have to sing and act but also rap! And that's not even mentioning the awesome aspect of putting a hip-hop spin on an opera written in French in 1875! What a challenge! But Beyoncé thought the music was absolutely wonderful and with the yes-yes-yes support of her Destiny's Child sisters, she accepted the role! "If it wasn't for my girls saying, 'Girl, you can

41

do it. You can do it,' I wouldn't have done it," said Beyoncé.

Spreading the Power

It should come as no surprise that the girls' positive vibe is also fueled by making music and continuing to get their message out into the world. They don't just take on projects or perform so they can put it on their résumé! They do it because they all adore music and it fuels their souls. As music lovers, of course they have lots and lots of faves, including Wyclef Jean, Stevie Wonder, the Jackson Five, Avant, and rapper Mase. As for fellow females who keep that independent vibe alive, D.C. groove on the Supremes, Lauryn Hill, TLC, En Vogue, Celine Dion, Whitney Houston, Jewel, and Janet Jackson, to name just a few.

In fact, at this year's American Music Awards, the girls were psyched to win for Favorite soul/R&B group, but they were super-psyched to be there to witness Janet Jackson receive a special award of merit for her awesome accomplishments in music and dedication to charity. They all thought it was really cool and that Janet totally deserved to be recognized for all her hard work and her amazing talents as an entertainer. Beyoncé told reporters backstage that the group absolutely loves Janet and that she's one of Destiny's Child's role models.

That explains partly why Kelly, Michelle, and Beyoncé joined up with MTV last March to help honor Janet in the new annual special *mtvICON*. If you happened to catch it, then you know that on the special, Destiny's Child, along with Macy Gray, 'N Sync, Outkast, Christina Aguilera, Britney Spears, Aaliyah, and other artists participated in the star-studded special tribute to honor Janet. Some of them were asked to perform a Janet song, too. Of course Destiny's Child was one of the artists who had such an honor. They did an awesome cover of Janet's "Let's Wait Awhile." In addition, the ladies talked about how their own music and lives have been influenced by Janet's fab music and spirit. Beyoncé, Kelly, and Michelle were thrilled to have the opportunity to let Janet know how much she inspired them while they were growing up. Certainly Ms. Jackson was pretty thrilled herself meeting the talented trio and watching them put a D.C. spin on one of her songs. It was a night to remember for everyone!

As Beyoncé, Michelle, and Kelly are inspired by other music artists, they are also inspired by their fans to keep up their hard work. The ladies go out of their way to take part in events and benefits that they hope will empower young people to go for it and reach for the stars. Last summer, the girls flew to New Orleans to perform at the Seventh Annual Essence Music Festival. The event showcased some of the hottest R&B, hip-hop, rap, and jazz artists around. You can bet the D.C. sweeties loved that, but they also dug the fact that there was an empowerment seminar featuring African-American artists, scholars, and leaders.

Even though they are super busy, Michelle, Kelly, and Beyoncé believe in participating in events such as the Essence Music Festival 'cause spreading the word about believing in your dreams and in yourself is one of Destiny's Child's key goals! Though taking on such "extra" commitments makes their schedule a little tighter, the girls are happy to do it! Now that's dedication!

CHAPTER 6

Jumpin' to the Top

1997: Destiny's Child signs with Columbia Records. "Killing Time" is released on the *Men in Black* soundtrack starring Will Smith and Tommy Lee Jones. Destiny's Child is flown to New York and other major cities to make in-store appearances with Will Smith, whose tunes "Men in Black" and "Just Cruisin'" also appear on the album.

1998: *Destiny's Child* is released. The single "No, No, No" shoots up the charts . . . The girls record "Get on the Bus" for the soundtrack *Why Do Fools Fall in Love? . . .* The group does lots of interviews with the press and plenty of performances, including touring with Boyz II Men.

1999: *The Writing's on the Wall* is released and "Bills, Bills, Bills" goes to number one on the U.S. charts in July. It also hits the top ten on the U.K. charts! "Bug A Boo" starts its climb and soon reaches number one!

2000: Destiny's Child continues touring to support *The Writing's on the Wall* . . . Members La-Tavia Roberson and LeToya Luckett part ways with Destiny's Child in the beginning of the year. Michelle Williams and Farrah Franklin join the group . . . Destiny's Child continues touring, opening for Christina Aguilera on her mega tour . . . In March, the single "Say My Name" shoots up the charts and soon hits number one! . . . In the late summer, Farrah leaves the group. Beyoncé, Michelle, and Kelly decide to keep Destiny's Child as a trio . . . "Jumpin' Jumpin'" marks D.C.'s fourth number one hit!

2001: Michelle, Kelly, and Beyoncé help ring in the New Year with Ideal, Jon B, and Shaquille O'Neal in downtown Los Angeles at the Staples Center . . . In February, Destiny's Child performs "Independent Women Part 1" and

"Jumpin' Jumpin'" in Washington, D.C. to mark President George W. Bush's move into the White House. Other guest performers include Ricky Martin, 98°, and Jessica Simpson . . . The MTV special *Making the Video "Survivor"* airs at various times throughout March, April, and May . . . Destiny's Child's third album, *Survivor*, drops in May . . . The threesome appears on various talk shows including *The Rosie O'Donnell Show* and *The Today Show* . . . The group wins the award for Favorite Singing Group at the Nickelodeon Kids' Choice Awards . . . Beyoncé stars as Carmen in MTV's *Carmen: A Hip Hopera* . . . Destiny's Child teams up with Candie's shoes to launch their vintage shoe line . . . The group headlines MTV's first *TRL* tour during the summer months. Wow! And the year's not over yet!

CHAPTER 7
Get Personal with the D.C. Sisters

It's pretty obvious that Beyoncé, Kelly, and Michelle are just like sisters! If there's ever a problem (and there rarely is!) the girls just sit down and have a heart-to-heart. They love one another very much, and they never want anything ever to come between them. That's why they see Destiny's Child being together for a long, long time to come!

Since Beyoncé and Kelly grew up together in Houston, there's a bond between them that is super special. Their family ties make them cousins, but really they're more like sisters. Ever since they were little, these two have been hanging together. "Personally, we're closer than most real sisters," says Kelly.

Not only that, but since the girls have been singing together forever, they totally are in tune with each others' voices. They know which part is right for the other, and also when their voices with Michelle's are coming together in perfect D.C. harmony. It was very exciting for the divas to share lead vocals on some of *Survivor*'s tracks, and there was no competition about who would sing what 'cause they're always thinking about what's best for Destiny's Child as a whole. It's one of the many ways the ladies keep their music real and strong!

If they ever happen to hit a bump in the road, then Michelle, Kelly, and Beyoncé know that they have one another to lean on. Just knowing this is a great comfort, especially when the ladies are far from home, jetting from gig to gig. The girls also hold hands and pray to boost spiritual strength and energy. They have an awesome connection, and afterward they feel much stronger to take on whatever the future might hold.

The three ladies also believe that honesty is the best policy when it comes to the group and their friendship. That's why Beyoncé, Kelly, and Michelle tell it like it is. When news broke that the girls were interested in doing some solo projects, a buzz started to spread that maybe the group was on the fritz and might call it quits. That couldn't have been farther from the truth! As far as Beyoncé, Michelle, and Kelly are concerned, they're just getting going with Destiny's Child and they have big hopes to continue for many years to come. In fact, they have always said that they want to be legends like the Supremes! So, by pursuing the solo stuff, the girls are NOT breaking up — they're just branching out!

Destiny's Child is down with change. That's why when the group members came and went, the girls forged ahead with Destiny's Child. All those changes were just a part of growing as a group and also as individual artists. Similarly, they don't ever want to hold one another back if an opportunity comes up for one of them. They know "solo" experiences will only feed back into Destiny's Child. Such growth helps keep their creativity pumpin' and their songs jumpin'!

This year, Beyoncé and Kelly both got their feet wet with some solo outings. As you already know, Beyoncé took on the challenging role as Carmen in MTV's *Carmen: A Hip Hopera*. Kelly made her solo debut back in February by recording the beautiful song "Angel" for the soundtrack to the flick *Down to Earth* starring funnyman Chris Rock. You can bet that Michelle was very proud of her D.C. sisters Kelly and Beyoncé.

Late last year, Beyoncé's dad, who helps manage the group, said that when Beyoncé, Kelly, and Michelle release solo albums, it will be at the same time, but they will be in different musical styles. He told reporters that Beyoncé will be in the pop/R&B arena, Kelly will be in alternative/R&B (think Lenny Kravitz) and Michelle will be in the gospel category. Michelle loves listening to gospel music and is looking forward to being able to sing what she describes as "R&B-tinged gospel." But Michelle also grooves on being a part of D.C. and she thinks it's pretty cool that she can do both. That's why as soon as they finish their solo gigs, the gals say they want to come back together and do another Destiny's Child album. Sounds like a great plan!

Aside from putting out a solo record someday, Beyoncé is also looking forward to doing a lot more songwriting in the time to come. Beyoncé wrote plenty for *Survivor*, but she's got a whole lotta awesome songs swimming around in her head and she hopes to write material for other artists real soon. "Writing for another artist's voice is going to be such a learning experience," she told *Billboard* magazine. Maybe she'll write some jammin' songs for her D.C. sisters' solo projects! We'll have to wait and see!

Destiny's Child Survivor Profile

BEYONCÉ
Full Name: Beyoncé Giselle Knowles
Birthdate: September 4, 1981
Grew Up: Houston, Texas
Hair: Light Brown/Blond
Eyes: Brown
Parents: Tina and Mathew
Birth Sign: Virgo
Fave Singers: Diana Ross, Stevie Wonder, Janet Jackson, Mariah Carey, Donny Hathaway
Makeup Must: Mascara and lip gloss
Fave Shoes: Really low stilettos for special occasions
Quote: "Deep down, I knew that we were going to make it past the bumps in the road and I knew we would be better as a result."
Status: SURVIVOR

KELLY
Full Name: Kelendria "Kelly" Trene Rowland
Birthdate: February 11, 1981
Grew Up: Houston, Texas
Hair: Black
Eyes: Brown

Mother: Doris
Birth Sign: Aquarius
Fave Singers: Whitney Houston, Janet Jackson, Diana Ross
Makeup Must: Powder
Fashion Fave: Anything with rhinestones
Quote: "The bond between us is very strong. It's deeper than just a singing group."
Status: SURVIVOR

MICHELLE
Full Name: Michelle Williams
Birthdate: December 1, 1980
Grew Up: Rockford, Illinois
Hair: Black
Eyes: Brown
Parents: Anita and Dennis
Birth Sign: Sagittarius
Fave Singers: Janet Jackson, Diana Ross
Makeup Must: Lipstick and powder
Fave Part of being in D.C.: Traveling, performing, and meeting the fans
Quote: "We help each other to not be scared, to be happy, and just glow."
Status: SURVIVOR

How Do You Rate?

Want to see how your stats stack up next to one of the decade's hottest groups? Go on! Don't be shy! Add your personal info below and see how you fit in with these R&B honeys!

Full Name: _____

Birthdate: _____

Grew Up: _____

Hair: _____

Eyes: _____

Parents: _____

Birth Sign: _____

Fave Singers: _____

Makeup Must: _____

Fashion Fave: _____

Fave Shoes: _____

Quote: _____

Fave Destiny's Child Album: _____

Fave Destiny's Child Song: _____

Fave Destiny's Child Video: _____

Fave Destiny's Child Member: _____

Fave Destiny's Child Show: _____

Fave Destiny's Child Lyric: _____

Fave Thing About Destiny's Child: _____

CHAPTER 8

D.C. Fly Facts to the Max

1. Back when the four original Destiny's Child girls were still children growing up in Houston, they used to try out routines in front of the customers at Beyoncé's mom's hair salon.

2. When Destiny's Child was getting their act together, they wanted to learn from the best. The girls listened to the music and studied the dance moves of such R&B legends as the Supremes, Chaka Khan, and the Jackson Five.

3. If you thought you recognized the title track from D.C.'s latest album *Survivor* from a TV commercial, you're right! "Survivor" played on a commercial for 1-800-CALL-ATT.

4. Destiny's Child has sold more than 15 million albums and singles worldwide!

5. Destiny's Child hopes that listening to *Survivor* will make people everywhere feel positive and free!

6. Beyoncé once said that their songs put a listener through an emotional roller coaster. Do they ever!

7. The gals have lent a helping hand by hooking up with lots of charities including Save The Music Foundation and the Elizabeth Glaser AIDS Foundation.

8. In 1999, Destiny's Child performed with 'N Sync, Wyclef, and Monica at a benefit for LIFEbeat, an HIV/AIDS-awareness organization.

9. Though the gals are well on their way to becoming superstars, believe it or not, they still get a little nervous sometimes before going on stage.

10. Did you know that Destiny's Child appeared on the *Britney Spears in Hawaii* TV special? It's true! The gals had a blast with Brit!

11. One of Kelly's all-time fave gospel singers is Shirley Caesar. She thinks she's awesome!

12. To promote "Killing Time" for the *Men in Black* soundtrack, the girls flew to the Big Apple and chilled with *MIB* star Will Smith at Tower Records. Later, they went to a party at Planet Hollywood and hung with Mary J. Blige, Puff Daddy, and Heavy D. You can bet the newcomers were psyched!

13. Beyoncé wrote all but four of the songs on Destiny's Child's new *Survivor* CD.

14. Michelle, Kelly, and Beyoncé are huge fans of Oprah Winfrey!

15. Before Destiny's Child, Beyoncé was in various groups including Girls Tyme, Something Fresh, Cliché, and Destiny.

16. Destiny's Child co-wrote four number one singles: "Bills, Bills, Bills," "Bug A Boo," "Say My Name," and "Jumpin' Jumpin'."

17. The gals of D.C. know one another's voices in-

side and out! They don't have any problem arranging their own harmonies!

18. "Beyoncé" is the maiden name of Beyoncé's mom, Tina.

19. Destiny's Child is managed by Beyoncé's father and the management company Music World Management.

20. "Independent Women Part 1" holds the highest airplay record of all time!

21. When Beyoncé was seven, she took home first place at a talent show after singing a moving rendition of John Lennon's "Imagine."

22. Some of the hotshots Destiny's Child has opened for include SWV, Dru Hill, Immature, Christina Aguilera, and Brian McKnight.

23. One of Beyoncé's best buds is her little sis and backup dancer, Solange.

24. Destiny's Child is the first American female group to debut at number one on the U.K. charts.

25. When Destiny's Child performed their new smash single, "Survivor" on the 2001 Soul Train Awards, Beyoncé was nervous that she'd forget the words, so she actually wrote some of the lyrics on her hand — just in case!

26. Destiny's Child recorded lots of versions and mixes of "Say My Name." The album version features basketball superstar Kobe Bryant! Destiny's Child did a song on Kobe's album first and then Kobe did the remix on D.C.'s album.

27. When *Survivor* dropped back in May 2001, it landed right at the top of the charts, and sold more copies in one week than any other album by a girl group!

28. On their debut album *Destiny's Child*, the crew of musical producers that the girls worked with included Wyclef Jean, Timbaland, and R. Kelly.

29. When the ex-host of *Star Search,* Ed McMahon, brought his web talent show nextbigstar.com to TV, Destiny's Child made a special guest appearance.

30. Destiny's Child was a name inspired by the

Bible's *Book of Isaiah*. The girls came up with Destiny, but since that name was already taken, they added "Child," to symbolize a rebirth of "Destiny."

31. As a foursome, Destiny's Child once made a cameo appearance on the TV show *The Smart Guy*.

CHAPTER 9

A Day in the Life of D.C.

If you had to come up with one word to describe a day in the life of Beyoncé, Kelly, and Michelle it would have to be BUSY! Certainly, there's never a dull moment for these ladies! Hey, being the hottest group going takes a lot of *doing* — time, energy, and let's not forget total dedication!

Even way back when Destiny's Child was just starting out, the girls' plates were pretty full. They were always serious about making a career for themselves in the world of music. That's no easy task considering how busy just school in itself keeps you. When the weekends came around, the girls were often practicing or performing. Summers were booked with a full-time training schedule that incorporated exercise routines with voice coaching and dance practice. Anywhere the girls could book a gig, you bet they did! Soon enough, when success tapped them on the shoulder, they were ready for it!

These days, now that Beyoncé, Michelle, and Kelly are done with school (though college could very well be on the horizon), they have plenty of other things going. Like what, you ask? Lots! Spend a day in the life of Destiny's Child and see for yourself!

Early to Rise

First of all, the trio and everyone involved with Destiny's Child are prepared to get up bright and early (sometimes the sun isn't even up yet!). An early call could be for a performance or interview on an early morning TV or radio show. They might have to get up early to catch a bus or a plane in order to do a performance or make an appearance at a benefit. Sometimes, the wee hours are used to finish up work in the studio. Whatever the business, rarely do Beyoncé, Kelly, and Michelle get to sleep in late and lounge around in their jammies. Well, unless they take a few days off of course!

Mid-Morning

By now, the girls have probably grabbed a quick breakfast, maybe some fruit and juice. Next up could be a video shoot for their next single. Before it's time to shoot the video, however, the concept of the video must be discussed and agreed upon with the director and designer. Some questions to answer include where the video will be shot, what it will look like, what the girls will be wearing, etc. If all of these things have been worked out, then it's time to get those cameras rolling!

After going through wardrobe and makeup, the girls arrive on the set and get ready to do their thing. It's a little different from singing live because they have to be aware of the cameras and also do dance moves that have probably been choreographed just for the video. Finishing a video might take a few takes or it could take more. It depends on lots of things, from the weather to the location. In any case, Beyoncé, Michelle, and Kelly have to be completely focused and in sync. Once the director thinks he has what he needs, the girls are off to their next appointment. All the hard work pays off in the end once the video is edited and ready to air. If you've seen Destiny's Child's past music videos, then you know a D.C. video is a delight for the senses!

The girls also could use this time to head into the studio and record new material, or if they've laid down the tracks already, they might get involved with doing mixes of a single, or other biz stuff.

Early Afternoon

Sometimes the group is on such a tight schedule that they can practically hear the clock ticking on a given day! Being on time for things takes careful planning and organization. That means if the girls have to catch a plane, then they'd better have their bags packed! They've got lots of people to help with the details, but it's up to Kelly, Michelle, and Beyoncé to be prepared for whatever the day holds. They have a lot of responsibilities on their shoulders.

What's next on the agenda? Well, it's not unheard of for the trio to jet clear across the country just so they can make an in-store appearance and sign autographs for their fans. Destiny's Child thinks they have some of the best, most loyal fans around, so it's a pleasure for them to be giving something back to those who have supported them through all these years. After signing autographs and taking pictures, the girls might be off to do any number of things, like a photo session for a magazine, an online chat, or maybe a rehearsal for an evening concert.

Then they might squeeze in a workout at the gym (they dig aerobics) and head back to the hotel. They don't get those awesome buff bods by just sitting around, that's for sure!

Sunset

The evening time could find Kelly, Beyoncé, and Michelle doing a sound check at the local theater or awards show venue where they will be performing. After their last-minute sound check, the girls are off to get dressed and look their best! Before going on, they might meet and greet backstage guests and answer questions from the press. Once it's time to go on, though, the girls get back together and try to focus on the upcoming performance. They might even say a little group prayer. When they take the stage, the audience explodes with cheers and Destiny's Child is pumped and ready to get the show on the road. This is a time when they can show their fans how grateful they are for their support, so D.C. gives each and every performance everything they've got! It's pure electric energy!

If it's a light night, then the trio might be chillin' at the hotel, having some good eats, gabbing about the stuff they did that day. There really is no such thing as off time, though, because if the trio has a free moment they take care of unfinished business such as returning phone calls, checking their e-mail, catching up with family. They also might go over tomorrow's schedule, or maybe even scribble down some lyrics to a song that might pop into their head.

Late to Bed

If they do a concert, afterward the girls sometimes hang with friends, fans, other music artists, and celebrities who are waiting backstage to say hello. By the time they get back to the hotel, it's usually pretty late. They're often beat, but that doesn't necessarily mean they fall right to sleep! Sometimes they stay up a while longer, talking about their performances, all the wonderful people that they met — basically processing everything that went down that day.

And when they finally say their prayers and slip under the covers, they fall fast asleep, dreaming sweet dreams!

Before they know it, the alarm goes off, and it's time to start another action-packed day on the Destiny's Child calendar!

A Day in the Life of . . . You!

Now that you know a little bit about what it can be like for Michelle, Kelly, and Beyoncé as members of Destiny's Child, what's it like to walk in your shoes for a day? Imagine you've just swapped places with one of the D.C. gals and you need to fill her in on what to expect to get through one of *your* days. School, walking the dog, chores, volleyball, chorus, your poetry group, updating your website, doing the dishes, homework, shopping, reading, writing, thinking — whatever you fill your time with, jot your schedule details right here. Bet you didn't realize how much stuff YOU get done in a day, did ya? Good for you!

My Schedule

6 a.m.: _____

7 a.m.: _____

8 a.m.: _____

9 a.m.: _____

10 a.m.: _____

11 a.m.: _____

12 p.m.: _____

1 p.m.: _____

2 p.m.: _____

3 p.m.: _____

4 p.m.: _____

5 p.m.: _____

6 p.m.: _____

7 p.m.: _____

8 p.m.: _____

9 p.m.: _____

10 p.m.: _____

11 p.m.: _____

12 a.m.: _____

CHAPTER 10

Tour Lore

If there's one thing that Michelle, Beyoncé, and Kelly love to do, it's perform. They consider this one of the biggest payoffs of being music artists.

They were barely out of diapers and bottles when the girls first got that singing feeling. Kelly started dreaming of being a singer when she was about four or five years old. She saw Whitney Houston on TV and told her mother that she wanted to sing. Ever since she was a little girl, Michelle's been singing gospel music. When she announced her plans to become a singer, her family said to go for it! Beyoncé decided on a career in music at a very young age as well. It was following her performance in a talent show. She was only four at the time, but she just loved the feeling of being on stage and knew singing was in the stars.

Even back in the early days, record executives were very impressed when they saw Destiny's Child perform. The girls were not only perfectly in sync vocally, but they were amazing in the footwork department, too! They've got this intense stage presence partly because the girls have been performing ever since they were little. Remember, the group formed when Kelly and Beyoncé were barely teenagers!

"It trips us out when we hear groups talk about how they feel like they are coming along because they have done six or seven shows," Kelly told a music magazine. "We have done so many, we can't keep track of them."

In fact, when they were starting out, Beyoncé said that even if there was just one person in the audience, they would perform. Hey, practice makes perfect!

It's kind of hard to imagine only one person showing up for a Destiny's Child concert these days! Their concerts sell out lickety-split! Their stage shows are fantastic, full of energy and awesome dance moves that leave the audience wanting more, more, more!

The last time the girls headed out on a major tour was back in 2000 when they toured with

Christina Aguilera. It was the first time they had a band onstage with them and they were really excited. The group had a blast and said that Christina was super-nice. "We've loved her since she's come out," said Kelly. "She's a wonderful performer." Christina was equally charmed! "I'm really a huge fan of Destiny's Child," Christina told MTV News. *"The Writing's on the Wall* was actually one of my favorite records I listened to all the time on tour."

The *Survivor* Tour

On the Destiny's Child *Survivor* tour, the trio will pull out all the stops. Since Michelle, Beyoncé, and Kelly spent a lot of time in the last year in the studio laying down the tracks for the new album, the three women are pumped to get out onstage to perform the songs. One of the reasons they love touring is because it gives *them* front row seats to the audience — they get to see how people respond to their music. It also gives the ladies a chance to connect with the fans on a personal level.

The *Survivor* tour will be huge, and Beyoncé, Kelly, and Michelle are ready to rock the world with their positive energy. The girls all have a lot of input when it comes to the choreography, backdrops, video displays and all the special effects you, the audience, see. Beyoncé, Michelle, and Kelly get *very* excited to see it all come together on stage. "You can't wait to give that to your fans," says Beyoncé.

There's no doubt about it — Destiny's Child's shows are bootylicious fantastic! They're full of silky smooth harmonies, awesome light displays, and unique choreography. When the girls take the stage, the audience members are on their feet in a jiffy and are groovin' to those feel-good rhythms!

As they travel around the globe, the ladies often don't get to go home for a while and they do sometimes miss it. In the early days, Beyoncé missed sleeping in her own bed. Now, she's used to hotel beds, but she still sometimes misses chillin' in her room back in Texas. Kelly says that even though they're not home much these days, they're still Houston girls.

But don't think the gals are complaining. Though Beyoncé, Michelle, and Kelly don't get to go home a lot, seeing how much joy their music brings to people is well worth it. They think that Destiny's Child fans are simply the best. Kelly says that D.C. fans have a wonderful way of making them feel right at home no matter what city they're in.

72

Oops! Onstage Mishaps

Though each concert is carefully planned, sometimes a surprise or two sneaks into the mix. Beyoncé shared in an online interview that one of her most embarrassing moments was when she slipped and fell down some stairs onstage. She said there were about thirty stairs and once she fell, she couldn't stop. She kept falling and falling and falling. At first, she didn't want to get up because she was so embarrassed, but of course she did. Luckily, Beyoncé didn't hurt herself. She brushed herself off and kept right on with the performance. The show must go on!

Another embarrassing moment happened when Destiny's Child was in Amsterdam performing at an awards show. It was the equivalent of the Grammys in the Netherlands and it was Michelle's first time being on television. As the girls were going through their dance routine, the back of Michelle's top popped open. Oops! Luckily, a fast-thinking dancer stood behind Michelle and snapped the top back together! "I kept smiling, she kept smiling," said Michelle. "It was all right." Actually, similar clothing mishaps have happened to Kelly and Beyoncé too. But all three girls are professionals and have learned to deal with such problems smoothly and quickly. Most people have no idea there's even something amiss!

One time that the audience definitely knew something was off, though, was when the lights went up and Kelly was sitting down onstage in a chair. Then the announcement came that poor Kelly had slipped and broken two toes backstage! It happened at the Magness Arena in Denver, Colorado, during the group's last days of touring with Christina Aguilera. Kelly was trying to do a quick costume change and it was kind of dark back there. She ended up slipping on a ramp and breaking the second and third toes of her right foot. Ouch!

Maybe other acts would have canceled the show, but not Destiny's Child! The girls didn't want to disappoint their beloved fans, so Kelly decided to sit out the dancing part of their performance. What a sweetheart! While she sang her vocals sitting on stage, Beyoncé's younger sister, Solange, stepped up and did Kelly's dance moves! What a cool idea! Fifteen-year-old Solange is not only a great dancer, but an awesome singer, too! She should be coming out with an album real soon. Till then, you can see Solange in Lil' Bow Wow's "Puppy Love" video.

Though Beyoncé and Kelly hadn't canceled a performance in nearly a decade, the group had to bow out of two shows at tour's end after Kelly's mishap. That gave Kelly the necessary break so her toes could heal. When they were all healed, Kelly was thrilled. She really missed dancing with her D.C. sisters, and you can bet Michelle and Beyoncé were glad to have Kelly back in good health, too!

If you haven't seen Destiny's Child in concert yet, what are you waiting for? They headlined the MTV *Total Request Live* tour in July, August, and September alongside Jessica Simpson, Dream, and 3LW. For a complete listing of upcoming *Survivor* tour dates, be sure to visit the Destiny's Child website and have a peek. The web address is listed in Chapter 15. There are many more D.C. performances to come, so be sure to get your tickets!

Whatever life on the road may hold for them, one thing is for sure: Destiny's Child sticks together through thick and thin! All three ladies have a great sense of humor and that certainly helps lighten the pressures of touring. When everything is said and done and these three honeys are back home, they'll certainly have plenty of great memories for their scrapbooks!

Blast From the Past

Think back on your own life and try to recall some of your fave memories. It can be something touching, empowering, or funny. Maybe it's when you scored the winning goal for your soccer team or when you ran for Student Council. Maybe it's when your grandparents told you about what it was like to be young in their days. From cooking a fancy meal for your parents' anniversary to coming face-to-face with your pen pal from another country, whatever you come up with, consider this your scrapbook and jot down some of your fondest memories here.

1. _____

2. _____

3. _____

4. _____

5. _____

CHAPTER 11
Destiny's Child Discography

Albums

Survivor, Columbia Records, 2001
1. "Independent Women Part I"
2. "Survivor"
3. "Bootylicious"
4. "Nasty Girl"
5. "Fancy"
6. "Apple Pie A La Mode"
7. "Sexy Daddy"
8. "Independent Women Part II"
9. "Happy Face"
10. "Emotion"
11. "Dangerously in Love"
12. "Brown Eyes"
13. "The Story of Beauty"

14. "Gospel Medley"
15. "Outro (DC-3) Thank You"

The Writing's on the Wall, Columbia Records, 1999
1. "Intro (The Writing's on the Wall)"
2. "So Good"
3. "Bills, Bills, Bills"
4. "Confessions" (featuring Missy Elliot)
5. "Bug A Boo"
6. "Temptation"
7. "Now That She's Gone"
8. "Where'd You Go"
9. "Hey Ladies"
10. "If You Leave" (featuring Next)
11. "Jumpin' Jumpin'"
12. "Say My Name"
13. "She Can't Love You"
14. "Stay"
15. "Sweet Sixteen"
16. "Outro (Amazing Grace)"

Destiny's Child, Columbia Records, 1998
1. "Second Nature"
2. "No, No, No Part 2" (featuring Wyclef Jean)
3. "With Me Part 1" (featuring Jermaine Dupri)
4. "Tell Me"

5. "Bridges"
6. "No, No, No Part 1"
7. "With Me Part 2" (featuring Master P)
8. "Show Me The Way"
9. "Killing Time"
10. "Illusion" (featuring Wyclef Jean/Pras)
11. "Birthday"
12. "Sail On"
13. "My Time Has Come"

Singles
"Survivor"
"Independent Women Part 1"
"Jumpin' Jumpin'"
"Say My Name"
"Bug A Boo"
"Bills, Bills, Bills"
"Get on the Bus"
"No, No, No"
"Killing Time"

Music Videos
"Survivor"
"Independent Women Part 1"
"Jumpin' Jumpin'"
"Say My Name"
"Bug A Boo"

"Bills, Bills, Bills"
"No, No, No"

Soundtracks

Film

Charlie's Angels, "Independent Women Part 1" and "DOT," 2000

Romeo Must Die, "Perfect Man," 2000

Big Momma's House, "Big Momma's Theme" with Da Brat & Vita, 2000

Life, "Stimulate Me" w/Mocha, 1999

Why Do Fools Fall in Love?, "Get on the Bus," 1998

Men in Black, "Killing Time," Sony/Columbia, 1997

TV

The PJ's, "No More Rainy Days," 1999

Other Recordings

Now That's What I Call Music Vol. 6, "Independent Women Part 1," 2001

Platinum Hits 2000, "Say My Name," 2000

Now That's What I Call Music Vol. 5, "Jumpin', Jumpin'," 2000

Another Rosie Christmas, "Spread A Little Love On Christmas Day," 2000

MTV Party to Go '99, "No, No, No Part 2," 1999

NFL Jams, "Once a Fool," 1998

Solo

Beyoncé Knowles: Sang "I Got That" with Amil on Amil's album, *All Money Is Legal*, 2000

Kelly Rowland: Sang "Angel" on the film soundtrack *Down to Earth*, 2001

CHAPTER 12

Beauty and Brains

Destiny's Child's look is as sizzling as their music. It radiates a confident vibe and plenty of heat! The styles Michelle, Beyoncé, and Kelly wear are totally unique and reflect their separate personalities. The three ladies never wear identical outfits, but there will often be one color or pattern that winds through each outfit so you can tell the girls are part of a group.

The ladies help in some of the designing, but Beyoncé's mother, Tina Knowles, is mainly behind Destiny's Child's awesome wardrobe. "She bases each outfit on the individual so we each have our own style, but we still look like a group," explained Beyoncé in an online interview. Sometimes, dresses are bought in threes and then recut and redesigned by Beyoncé's mom. Mrs. Knowles will be working on a clothing line soon, so if you like Destiny's Child's clothes, be on the lookout for her D.C.-inspired fashions to pop up in a store near you soon!

Though they have a stylist, Kelly, Beyoncé, and Michelle still love to shop. Michelle says she really enjoys shopping with her D.C. sisters 'cause they give her advice about what looks good on her. Beyoncé says that when she and Kelly go shopping, they end up shopping for each other more than themselves. Rather than competing with one another the girls compliment one another! Beyoncé believes that lack of communication and jealousy are often the reasons why female groups don't stay together. That's not happening with Destiny's Child because these three know that when they help each other look their best, it makes the whole group look and feel sooo good!

As for particular clothing, Beyoncé says that they don't really stress about brand name clothing. Whether they get it at a resale shop or at a brand name shop is not as important as if a piece looks good on or not. If Beyoncé had to name her style, she'd probably say it's urban/rock. She also thinks shimmery clothes and makeup look great when the lights hit them just right. Michelle likes Gucci and Fendi goods, while Kelly loves anything with rhinestones. When it comes to fave shopping places, Beyoncé says that Paris is tops on her list. Once, when the girls were short on time and they were given the choice of either eating or shopping, they chose to SHOP! "We were starving, but we had some clothes," said Beyoncé.

At awards shows last year, the trio glammed it up in outfits ranging from elegant green sequined evening gowns to more urban flavored gear. Whatever the choice, the gals always show plenty of first-class flair.

Though it's important for Destiny's Child to wear fresh and original outfits, they never sacrifice their self-respect. "Nasty Girl" on *Survivor* tells a little bit about how they feel about maintaining dignity while still looking good and keeping up with fashion trends. Michelle says that "Nasty Girl" is about "a not-so-classy girl" who walks out of the house wearing a way skimpy getup. "We love to wear shorts and skirts, but it's got to be tasteful," says Michelle. The group hopes "Nasty Girl" will let young women out there know there's nothing wrong with being sassy, but you've got to dress in a tasteful way.

The *Survivor* track "Bootylicious" has a similar message about being beautiful but with class. The lyrics and beats advise young people everywhere to be confident so their unique beauty will radiate from the inside out. If you feel good on the inside, then you just glow!

Beyoncé's mom Tina is also responsible for the trio's fab hairstyles, from Kelly's short-'n'-cute crop, to Michelle's sleek tresses, to Beyoncé's signature blond highlights. The girls believe in using plenty of conditioner to keep their hair healthy. Mrs. Knowles told a fashion magazine that black hair tends to be dry and fragile and that constant high-lighting could be damaging. That's why she came up with the idea of bonding platinum highlights to the strands around Beyoncé's face. The result? Standout gorgeous! Anyone can have Beyoncé's look now — she's modeling the hair color in ads for L'Oréal's Féria!

To have those glowing complexions, Beyoncé, Michelle, and Kelly don't do anything out of the or-dinary. When they wash their faces, they do make sure to wash *all* the makeup off thoroughly though because it can end up clogging pores. Beyoncé also recommends using an astringent or something sim-ilar to make sure every last dab of makeup is gone. Michelle uses several products, including Neutro-gena and Proactive to cleanse her face. Kelly says that she's a firm believer in facials. She loves to get them and says that they're totally relaxing.

They've Got Smarts!

Kelly, Beyoncé, and Michelle not only score high marks for style and good looks, but these three lovelies also rate tops in the smarts department too! Education has been a priority for the ladies ever since they were tots. Though they had big dreams of being singers someday, they knew that getting an education was just as important. Beyoncé and Kelly combined their love of singing with getting an education by attending a performing arts school in Houston. There they were able to pursue their dream by taking voice classes while staying in school. When the group started becoming successful, the girls were tutored at home. It was just like going to school, though more intense in some ways because they would have one-on-one time with their teachers. Imagine that — just you and your teacher hittin' the books!

Stressing about school? Beyoncé's advice is to talk to a friend if you've got a problem. She believes that it's important to get it out rather than running away from it. She also says that jogging or doing aerobics helps her to relieve stress.

Kelly says if you have a problem with a particular subject, that you shouldn't be afraid to ask someone for help. It can be scary, sure, but that's how you learn. Sometimes Kelly found math confusing, but she didn't give up. She stuck with it until she understood. "Just ask questions about it, and they can be answered," she says.

Michelle adds that it's also important to be able to talk to your parents openly and honestly. Another bit of advice? It might help to keep a diary and write down your thoughts. "One day you can maybe turn that into a song or a poem," she says. What a great idea!

It wasn't easy juggling school with a full-time music career, but these three did it. That's why they're firm believers that if you really put your mind to something, you can succeed no matter how difficult it may seem or how many obstacles come in the way.

In their early days, Destiny's Child even went on an "I Attend Tour" where they visited schools and urged kids to continue their education. The group performed and chatted with young people about the importance of getting a diploma so they can start making their dreams come true.

More recently, Destiny's Child, along with Wyclef Jean, Whitney Houston, Eric Clapton, and other artists performed at New York's Carnegie Hall in a benefit that celebrated the last century of American music. The concert took place earlier in 2001 and was organized by D.C.'s buddy Wyclef. The money from the concert went to the Wyclef Jean Foundation, which was set up to aid musical education for kids all over the world.

Beyoncé, Kelly, and Michelle had a lot of fun teaming up with Wyclef for such a worthy cause. They respect him so much because not only is he talented, but he also believed in Destiny's Child when it was first starting out. In past interviews, the group credited Wyclef for his awesome mixing abilities as well as for having taught them a thing or two about how to give high-energy performances.

When *Teen People* selected Beyoncé as one of the top "20 Teens Who Will Change the World," it wasn't just because Beyoncé is gorgeous and a great singer! It was for the whole package! Beyoncé is not only intelligent and well-spoken, but she's devoted practically her whole life to helping people feel good about themselves. Beyoncé's lyrics are written to inspire people to have more positive out-looks on the world so their lives will be more fulfilling. When she found out she was selected by the magazine, Beyoncé was very touched. She said in an online chat that of any of the awards Destiny's Child has received, making the "Teens Who Will Change the World" list was very important to her. She was not only proud to have been singled out from other music artists and celebrities in her age group, but also to be included among teens who were doing such remarkable things as coming up with cures for diseases and giving back to the community. "I was very, very honored," said Beyoncé.

Beyoncé shares this and many other honors she receives individually (her songwriting and producing Grammy nominations for instance) with Kelly and Michelle. They've got her back, and that gives her the gusto to go for it!

Beyoncé also credits her success to her family. They've believed in her dream of pursuing a career in the music business ever since she was little. She and her sister Solange are very close, and Beyoncé draws a lot of strength from their special bond. Beyoncé's father has been managing the group for a long while and also made sure Beyoncé didn't grow up too fast. Finally, Beyoncé's mother supports Destiny's Child by helping out with the D.C. wardrobe and hairstyling. Not only that, but often the whole Knowles family is on hand while the girls are touring to give them support.

It's very comforting for the group to have such a solid support system backing them wherever they go. "The great thing about Destiny's Child is that we have family on the road with us, so they check us if we ask for something ridiculous," said Beyoncé in an online chat. "They keep us grounded, and we keep each other grounded. We know that this can be taken away from us in a second, so we know to appreciate everything and be positive at all times." Right on!

CHAPTER 13
Spell Their Name

Spell their name, spell their name . . . you don't have to be queen or king of the spelling bee to know that Destiny's Child rocks! Here are just a few of the reasons why. . . .

D is for **D**eliver 'cause that's what Destiny's Child does whenever they make a date with their fans. Michelle, Kelly, and Beyoncé are extremely professional and they not only make a point of being on time, but they are totally present — body, mind, and soul!

E is for **E**motion 'cause Beyoncé, Michelle, and Kelly are always striving to sing from their hearts!

S is for **S**tylin' 'cause these chicks are as sassy as the music they make!

T   is for **T**ogether 'cause Beyoncé, Kelly, and Michelle are a tightly knit trio and they not only dig singing together, but they also love hanging together!

I   is for **I**nventive 'cause D.C.'s layered harmonies, awesome song beats, and funky fresh fashion sense are totally one-of-a-kind creations!

N   is for **N**ice 'cause though these ladies have been in the music business for oodles of years, they're still down-to-earth and super sweet!

Y   is for **Y**ou 'cause the success of Destiny's Child is reflected in the dedication of fans just like you!

S   is for **S**urvive 'cause it wasn't always easy going through the ups and downs of the music biz, but the gals held tight to their dreams and never stopped believing in themselves!

C   is for **C**lassy 'cause Destiny's Child always looks A-class and A-list with their unique sound and look!

H   is for **H**ouston 'cause that's where Destiny's Child originally got their start.

I   is for **I**n 'cause Destiny's Child is one of the hottest groups of the new millennium!

L is for **L**ight 'cause a room just lights up when Kelly, Michelle, and Beyoncé walk into it! They radiate confidence and beauty!

D is for **D**edicated 'cause Destiny's Child has made it their life's work to totally dedicate themselves to empowering the world with their powerful and positive music!

Buddy Dubbin'

Now that we've had some fun with letters, let's keep it going! Can you come up with some names for the group of pals that you like chillin' with? Have a slumber party and brainstorm! Then write down what you dub your group of buds here! If you get stuck, read a word or two off this list out loud and see if it doesn't get those ideas rolling!

Awesome	Girls	Nifty
Best	Hipster	Okay
Chums	Intense	Palz
Def	Jammin'	Quite
Elite	Kids	Right
Exciting	Lookin'	Sonic
Fly	Mighty	Super

Terrific   Very   Youth
Unique   Wow   Zippy

_____   _____

_____   _____

_____   _____

_____   _____

_____   _____

_____   _____

_____   _____

_____   _____

_____   _____

_____   _____

_____   _____

_____   _____

_____   _____

_____   _____

CHAPTER 14
Girl Power

This might sound kinda opposite, but Destiny's Child gets energy from spending energy! These three lovelies have no intention of slowing things down any time soon. "Now that we have had some success, we will work even harder," says Beyoncé. "We owe that to our fans."

The girls know how important it is to have good role models for young people. They really looked up to people like Diana Ross, Janet Jackson, and Whitney Houston when they were growing up. When they got to meet Diana at VH1's *Divas 2000: A Tribute to Diana Ross*, the girls were overcome with emotion. Beyoncé said in an interview that there were tears in their eyes. "I know I saw Diana Ross on my left and Mariah Carey, and those were the people that we've always dreamed of meeting and being like," said Beyoncé. "That's something we will never forget."

Something else Beyoncé and Kelly will never forget is when the female R&B group SWV took them aside and gave them advice about the music biz when they were first starting out. Beyoncé and Kelly said that the SWV women were like big sisters to Destiny's Child and they really appreciated the fact that they took the time to let them know they believed in them.

Today, Beyoncé, Michelle, and Kelly know that lots of young people are looking up to Destiny's Child too. That's why they work so hard to give back by making such inspiring music and by setting a good example. They believe that you have to *be* positive in order to be positive role models.

Now that D.C. knows plenty about the ups and downs of the music biz firsthand, they've made a point of looking out for other up-and-coming groups. Destiny's Child has carried the sisterly torch by being "big sisters" to PYT, a foursome of fifteen-year-old girls. They had plenty of time to share their wisdom since PYT was scheduled to join them on their *Survivor* tour.

Of course Michelle, Beyoncé, and Kelly were busy, but they made time because they feel it's all part of their musical and spiritual responsibility. Destiny's Child is all about staying true to the soul and helping make dreams come true!

The Secret Behind the Success

As for those fans who dream of being like them someday, Destiny's Child says that it's important to take action and stay connected to the spiritual. The girls' advice: Get involved. Stay true to yourself. Try to be different, but not too different.

Though Destiny's Child knows the importance of having family and friends close by so you can lean on each other, they also know the value of being independent women! "I think the hazard of being a young woman in this business is that people assume you're being led around by others — mostly men," Beyoncé told *Billboard* magazine. "That's far from the situation that we're in."

Beyoncé says that "Independent Women Part 1" is intended to be an anthem to all the women in the world who stand on their own two feet without needing a man to hold them up. Judging from the awesome success of the single, it's a sure thing that women all over the world heard Beyoncé's message loud and clear! With "Independent Women Part 1,"

Destiny's Child made women everywhere feel the power of female unity and pride. You go, girls!

What is the secret behind Destiny's Child's positive power? They just focus on the future and try not to dwell on the past or be weighed down by regret and negative vibes. Though it's hard dealing with criticism, the girls say that it's important to be secure with yourself and stay positive.

Beyoncé says that she gains strength from praying. And when she wants to leave the concerns of the world behind, she relaxes by lighting candles and listening to R&B singer and composer Donny Hathaway.

As of now, Michelle, Beyoncé, and Kelly are all single. They know there's plenty of time for dating and boyfriends in the future. Right now, their priority is Destiny's Child and to keep making great music. When asked if they had any dating advice, Beyoncé said that you should always be yourself and not try to impress anybody. Sounds right on!

There's no doubt that with their talent and optimistic outlook, Beyoncé, Kelly, and Michelle are going to be making beautiful music together for a long, long time to come! They thank their fans from the bottom of their hearts for all the support they've given Destiny's Child over the years. Says

Kelly, "God bless and know that you can do anything if you put your minds to it."

Shining Bright

Destiny's Child is all for the power of love and taking positive action! In this section, answer some of these questions about you and your circle of friends and see what keeps that positive energy flowing fast!

1. What are some of the things that keep you and your circle of friends together?

_____

_____

_____

2. What have you done in the past that made you feel independent?

_____

_____

_____

3. What bit of advice did you receive from someone that made you feel good about yourself?

_____

_____

_____

4. What is some advice you would give to a younger person to inspire them to keep believing in their dreams?

_____

_____

_____

5. What are some things about your personality that make you a Survivor with a capital "S"?

_____

_____

_____

CHAPTER 15

Show 'Em You Care

If you're a fan of Destiny's Child, let them know how much you care! The best way to connect with the group is to log onto their website and catch up with what's going on in Beyoncé, Kelly, and Michelle's busy lives.

You can get the scoop on Destiny's Child through several web addresses. The Columbia Records website is located at *www.columbiarecords. com*. There's a link on the Columbia site that will lead you to *www.destinyschild.com* where you'll find lots more about what's new with the group, including info about Destiny's Child's latest releases, a calendar listing future TV appearances, video clips, and a hot image gallery. There's also a store where you can buy Destiny's Child's albums and singles.

You can find the Official Fan Club Website For Destiny's Child at *www.dc-unplugged.com*. There's lots of great info about the group here as well, including a Chat Room where you can connect with other Destiny's Child fans. Have a message for Michelle, Beyoncé, and Kelly that you want the world to see? Then just pop into the DC Forum and post your thoughts or questions on the message board.

You can also send the gals e-mail at *FANMAIL@musicworldentertainment.com* and tell them how their music has touched your life! Remember, the song "The Story of Beauty" was inspired by a fan letter the girls received, so that proves they do read their mail. Always remember that you should ask a parent for permission before sending any personal info over the Internet. Be safe!

CHAPTER 16

Destiny's Child Quiz Biz

Okay, number one Destiny's Child fans, let's see how much info about Destiny's Child you've soaked up. That's right, it's time for a little pop quiz! Don't worry — all of the answers can be found somewhere in the previous pages of this book. Try your hand at the following 15 true or false questions and see which ones you can ace. Good luck and peace out!

1. **The name of the first single from Destiny's Child's new album, *Survivor*, is "Survivor."**
2. **"Independent Women Part 1" is featured on the soundtrack for the film *Crouching Tiger, Hidden Dragon*.**

3. Destiny's Child performed at tributes to Diana Ross and Janet Jackson.
4. Michelle grew up in Houston, Texas.
5. Beyoncé's little sister, Solange Knowles, designs the awesome fashions that the group wears onstage.
6. Destiny's Child's first hit single, "Killing Time," was featured on the soundtrack for the film *Spy Kids*.
7. Sometimes, if there's a problem, Michelle, Kelly, and Beyoncé pray together to gain strength to overcome it.
8. In 2000, the girls toured with Christina Aguilera.
9. The single "Emotion" from *Survivor* was written by '70s sensations the Bee Gees.
10. Beyoncé, Kelly, and Michelle have teamed up with Candie's to sell *Survivor* gumballs.
11. Though Destiny's Child was nominated for five Grammys in 2001, they didn't win any.
12. Basketball superstar Kobe Bryant appears on a version of the hit single "Say My Name."

13. *Teen People* selected Beyoncé as one of the top "20 Teens Who Will Change the World."
14. The D.C. gals only wear expensive designer clothing.
15. Destiny's Child is inspired by lots of different types of musical styles.

D.C. QUIZ ANSWERS

1. **True**
   The first single from Destiny's Child's latest album is "Survivor."
2. **False**
   "Independent Women Part 1" is featured on the soundtrack for the film *Charlie's Angels*.
3. **True**
   Destiny's Child was honored to be part of mtvICON honoring Janet Jackson and VH1's *Divas 2000: A Tribute to Diana Ross*.
4. **False**
   Michelle grew up in Rockford, Illinois, which is near Chicago. Kelly and Beyoncé grew up in Houston.
5. **False**

Beyoncé's mother, Tina Knowles, designs Destiny's Child's gorgeous outfits and also styles the ladies' hair.

6. **False**

"Killing Time" was featured on the soundtrack for the Will Smith flick *Men in Black*.

7. **True**

Destiny's Child believes in the power of prayer.

8. **True**

Destiny's Child toured with Christina Aguilera. They're big fans of one another's music.

9. **True**

"Emotion" was penned by Bee Gees brothers Maurice and Barry Gibb. It was a huge hit back in 1978.

10. **False**

Destiny's Child teamed up with Candie's to sell shoes, not gumballs!

11. **False**

Destiny's Child took home two Grammys this year: one for Best R&B Performance by a Duo or Group With Vocal for "Say My Name" and a second one for Best R&B Song for "Say My Name."

12. **True**

   The album version of "Say My Name" features Kobe belting it out with Destiny's Child!

13. **True**

   Beyoncé said that making the "20 Teens Who Will Change the World" list was one of her biggest honors.

14. **False**

   The girls wear what looks and feels good on them. It doesn't matter if it's designer or not!

15. **True**

   All sorts of music including pop, gospel, hip-hop, and R&B inspire Beyoncé, Kelly, and Michelle.